NIGHT WATCH

A TIMELESS CHRISTMAS STORY
BY PAUL DARCY BOLES

ILLUSTRATED BY NORM KOHN

Published by
PEACHTREE PUBLISHERS, LTD.
494 Armour Circle, N. E.
Atlanta, Georgia 30324

Manufactured in The United States
of America.

LC-80-8778
ISBN: 0-931948-15-0

Below decks in the second bank of rowers we knew we had been in a battle—and a storm following battle; yet that was all we knew. And who keeps count of battles? Or storms?

The life is that of an animal chained to a post. I, Voldi, must have been a useful animal. For I had lived, I had survived. By the calculations in my head—though sometimes they went wrong—I thought I had been a galley rower for almost a year.

As I say, it is hard keeping tally. At first when you are flung below and they lock the circles of iron around your wrists there is still pride. The pride of knowing your name, where you came from. The pride of remembering how a girl's face looked and the wine jars smelled and the dust of the road moved in the sunlight. When the pride begins to go a different desperation sets in. I have no words to tell of that other terror. Those who have been in the galleys know what truth I speak.

Oh, at first, like all the rest, I had cherished notions of escape. For the galley in which I served was not unusual. It was designed for fighting and that alone; as we Greeks had first designed such galleys for Salamis—and Salamis was 480 years before. It was a vessel of war, slim and long. Below it was packed with rowers. The light upper deck held the soldiery. They had their shields, their bows and arrows, their spears—they had their kind of freedom. When the engagements came, no matter how close to death and complete madness you might be in the rowing banks, there was the chance, small but beautiful, of possible escape.

There were stories of such escape. The old man, the one we called the Bear—gods, he was full of stories! He sat ahead of me in my rowing bank. We were two of fifty-two men on that tier. In the mornings when the first light stole over the water and touched the dark wooden rim of the rowing port beside him I could always see first of all his shoulders, which were enormous; his long, thick hair, grizzled like a great bear's pelt; the way his huge head sat on the column of his neck. If it was a time when the drumbeats of the timekeepers in the bow had slackened to a slow pulsing count or nearly died out, we would talk a little. The timekeepers, who beat out on their heavy-skinned drums the rhythm of the strokes, were called the duumvir. I have thought that they were only men performing their given task. Yet to me it was the concentration of all evil. The very name, duumvir, is Roman; oh, yes, they had adopted our Greek ships, our ways of fighting, our certain wisdom. In the old days it was Themistocles the

8

Athenian who had placed faith in the wooden walls of our triremes and who had magnificently defeated the Persians and all of Xerxes' might at Salamis! But now we had worse than a Persian fleet to conquer. Now we were slaves.

So, when I heard those strokes of the duumvir's mallets on their drums, my teeth would grind together as though I had already gone mad. It was not until I saw the light seeping in the port to touch the Bear's dignity—even naked, he possessed dignity; a hillman, he'd been, one of those who work their little crop even as Ulysses did in the golden days before war or our gods' wrath—that I could know the joy of remembering that I was, after all, still alive. And that there might still be freedom.

So we would manage to talk, the Bear and I, in those mornings. The old Bear would turn his head slowly, until I could see the brightness of one black eye. "Voldi," he would say in his gruff, half-croaking hillman's speech. "It was thirty-one years ago, I was thinking, Voldi, that the battle of Actium took place. Ah, Voldi, I was a young man then; as young as you are."

I would say, "I am not young. My hands are as old as yours, old man. I have held this oar so long my hands are grown to it. I have smelled filth and eaten bad bread and looked squinting into blackness so long I am as old as you are. I have forgotten what it is to be young."

He would laugh, a soft laugh yet harsh because of his cracked voice. "You are yet a child, for no aging philosopher could contain that bitterness. But, Voldi, I wish to tell you: I heard the news of Actium from a

9

running messenger, four days after the event. How it stirred me! Antony against Octavian, you recall—using machines that had immense springs in them, mounted on huge wooden towers on the upper decks. The machines threw darts and boulders. But what impressed me most—"

"Antony lost that battle," I said with relish. "And who cares, when Roman fights Roman, what the outcome may be?"

"Yes, it is a child," he would say, nodding. "A child's answer. What impressed me most, Voldi, was the interesting number of galley slaves who escaped. The messenger said they had worked in concert, taking advantage of the confusion to tear up their benches—"

"And if they did, old man?" I would say softly. For the Bear when he spoke in this vein made my heart turn in my chest—in a galley it is not good to let yourself be excited too much; it brings on the madness. A dozen men had gone mad in the time of my slavery. As soon as their madness was accredited by the overseers—who whipped them to make sure they were not shamming—they were slain, then cut up with short-swords and flung through the sweep ports.

"It has been done, Voldi," he would say in his quiet husk of a voice. "It has been accomplished. Think on that."

Now we had been in a battle and in a storm afterward. The galley was removed from the bulk of the fleet; we'd been blown off course by the storm—I'd heard the officers shout it in the confusion. The memory of the battle, like ten battles before it, moved through my muscles. Once during the tumult I'd had the notion that in the screaming and the clamor of ship against ship we would, this time, go under. Yet we had not gone under; perhaps we'd won the battle.

It was night—what time I could not tell, though as a rule from the look of the water you could read the approximate times of night or day. In the hour of midnight the water would be a clear deep blue—unless we were near shore, or shoals, when it would change to a cold green. If there was a moon you could nearly tell by the light of it on the water—though you could seldom see the moon herself—what the hour might be. Yet now, though it was light out, I could not read the signs.

I will tell you: it was a strange night. I have never known a stranger one. Nor could I tell what had wakened me. After battle, or storm, or both, the overseers—and the officers, and the captain above them—have grace enough to let the rowers rest. It is a small rest, short and uneasy, filled, as all our sleep was filled, by the sudden moans of men whose very sleep is riddled by fear; by the slow sound of chains, shifting with tumbled human bodies; by the steady, undying sound of the Roman duumvir's drums. For when one pair of duumvir ceases, another takes over in its stead, and they do not miss a stroke. They were counting now, only, for the stern sweep—all other oars trailed silent; lifting myself a little, I could see the froth line along my oar blade.

The second of straining to see gave me another strange thought. It was of all the fish and the water animals in a night like this one; how pleasing it was for them to be free and unafraid! Just before the storm, while we were still shaking from the battle—when the overseers were inspecting us to see how many dead we had—many birds had come rushing by. Through the groans of the dying, through the splashes as the bodies fell into the water, we below decks had heard the birds. For one instant I had seen them through the sweep port as they passed in a cloud—and then, I recalled, I had felt as now. There was something in me which went out and out to the tameless wonder of fish, sea animals and birds. Of course, they'd been merely the harbingers of storm, running before it like ships of the air rowed by their wings. Yet the feeling that remained was the same I got often from the old man called the Bear. And suddenly, as I watched, I saw that the old man also was awake, for he turned his head to me.

"Voldi," he said. There was that in his voice which had been there before. But it was stronger now. It was the strongest I had ever heard it. In spite of myself I felt my heart leap up and begin beating hard against the smooth-worn heavy grip of my oar.

"Yes," I whispered. "Old man, I am awake."

"Of course," he said in that throaty, creaking murmur. "What wakened you?"

"Oh, old man, who knows? Hunger, perhaps. They fed us before battle. It seems a long time ago." I paused and then went on. "It is a miracle, old man, that I have developed a liking for their coarse bread and warm water. Is not that a miracle? For I was always a careful chooser of food and drink."

"No matter," he said. The eye was yet turned

12

toward me; in the pale glimmer—it might have been moonlight, though I had never observed moonlight so clear and searching as this—the eye blazed with life. I wanted to tell him he seemed to me in that instant as young as any man I had ever known. But it was no place to bandy compliments, and I had my defenses to think of. For, I have thought since then, when men are trapped together—in war, in slavery, in darkness—each must keep his own invisible shield up at all times. When the shield drops away he is worse than naked; he is at the mercy of his emotions. And we Greeks, before the Romans, had learned to keep those emotions in harness. Before they stole our bodies and our truths, we were men. It was still possible to be a man if one kept the shield.

"No matter, Voldi," the old Bear was saying. I could scarcely hear him; yet the words seemed to burn my bones. "There is other food and drink. What has wakened you had wakened me. Now think." All was quiet again—only the rustle of the waters, the creak of the stern sweep and, somewhere above, a soldier laughing softly. No doubt he'd be congratulating himself on having come through another battle and a severe storm. My teeth ground together despite myself and I said, whispering hard, "I think, old man. Sometimes I think too much."

"No," he said strongly. "Think. Have you ever smelled air like this before? Or seen light like this before?"

Gradually then his words—they still seemed in my bones like fire—took hold. I turned my face to the sweep port; though I didn't raise myself again, yet as I examined the quality of the light falling through there, I could see that he was right. It was fluid as melted silver; yet it held something else. When I was a child I had observed light like that. It had been long ago, when I was seated with my father and mother and brothers, just beside the white wall of our home. The stars had been out, and each shape of bush and tree and path rim and leaf had been clearly outlined.

Cautiously, as one might test the edge of a cliff before crawling outward to an eagle's nest, I smelled the air. And again the feeling of wonder and strangeness filled me, for the air was different.

My nostrils contracted then. I said softly, "Old man, it is only that we are near land. Those are the land smells."

"Yes, land. And what else?"

Rage filled me. My hands tightened on my oar grip.

"What else must there be? Signs and portents, visions and wonders? Old man, old Bear," I said cruelly, for I could feel the shield slipping a little and I must hold it high. "One morning soon the overseers will come here and find you smiling at them. Or discover you trading your joyful words for a moment of happiness. Then they will kill you; one blow—as hale as you are, one blow. Then the short-sword and the fishes. It would amuse them. And I will tell you this, old one"—I was leaning forward, the oar grip pressing my chest—"they are fools, but in this they will be right. When there is no chance for truth to exist, to mention its name in faith and trust is a sin. It is a black sin."

I realized then that he was laughing and my rage could not hold back. He was laughing softly, but it

14

was a real laugh. I said, "I speak as a Greek, not a soft-headed believer in hearth idols." I lifted my hands; the chained wrists felt my anger, blood pounding in them. "Let your words cut these, old man."

Even as I spoke, he had ceased laughing; and now, I thought, our friendship, such as it had been, would also stop. For I'd seen it happen before; for a time, two men would strike up a mumbled acquaintance here below. They would tell each other where they came from, their family name, and would confide small details of a past which was all they possessed. That was all very well, but what they did not know—could not know, as they grasped at these straws of comfort—was that regret and the pain of regret's poison began destroying them. Soon they would go mad, or at the least become implacable enemies. It was better if they had been enemies from the start, I had thought; for then they possessed shields, and these and these only could save them.

But the Bear was not offended. He was still looking as far toward me as his great head could turn.

"Yes, Voldi. By your lights you are a Greek. By mine you are a man and somewhat of a thinking man; one who deserves better of life than this. I think we are near shore. That much is true."

On the opposite tier of benches a man began howling like a dog gone mad, and those around him wakened and cursed; chains clanked, and the benches made that shifting sound that comes when many men stir in the agony of being wakened. From above there was a sharp word, and the sounds of footfalls on the short stair; peering along the aisle,

15

suffering the fetid stench which was worst there, I could see the feet and legs of an overseer. But he came no farther, only remained crouched in the entryway, eyes shining in the light of an oil lamp.

The man who had been taken by nightmare quickly ceased his noise—it trailed off into a series of whimpers and then stopped utterly. Somebody on the first bank of rowers cursed the overseer, voice low but savage. I could hear the overseer laugh. It was a satisfied laugh. He slapped his whip at the wall of the hatchway; it made a sound like an oar breaking. Then he went up again, footfalls soft and softer.

Somehow sight of him had made solid the weight in my chest. It was not my heart, though that was beating almost richly enough to suffocate me. It was something else, part of what I have called my shield, perhaps; I do not know what it was. But it was as heavy with depth as a boulder no man could move. "There," I whispered. "So much for being near shore. Break him, Bear. Remove him, as you would cut my chains with words."

"Not words alone," said the Bear; and this time he made a forward motion with his head. I leaned close, the oar grip digging again into my chest muscles, and the old man said, "Words and very simple action. Now, Voldi, listen."

I understood as I listened that I had never truly listened before. Oh, I had thought of his words; had considered what he had told of that battle of Actium, in which Antony lost to Octavian, and in which, more vastly important to me, galley slaves had gone free. But what had an event thirty-one years past to do with the present? Yet, as he spoke now, all I had worked to put down and forget rose up again in me; I must confess it, I was no true Greek then. My veins began working with a yeast of triumph; it seemed to me, with one part of my person, that madness lay just beyond the next thought. My thoughts richened and grew like a boy's when he thinks for the first time of the world before him, with its infinite chances.

I could feel the shield slip and slip; I grunted, nodded from time to time, attempted—in a desperate clutch after the slipping shield—to throw dark reason into his shining plan. Yet I could not. And it was not all so unreasonable. There was a drunkenness in me, though I had not had a draught of unmixed wine for more than a year; there was a feeling of forward-going, as though something that shone in the light were about to release me like an arrow. When I heard this thing, I thought the old man was a kind of sorcerer; so simple was the plan, yet it needed so much to assist it.

So he talked on, while the light shone and the drumbeats sounded; craning there, I had ceased to protest even with grunting objections. Again as we sat in that clear light from the ports I thought, beneath the sense of his words, of my past life; of the way the grass had shone beneath my sandals. Of the temple where my mother had gone on the holy days to make little sacrifices for the peace and health and joy of our family; of the colonnades, some of them broken, others proud, of our ancient places of worship. The voices of the Romans at their games were like the voices of crows; but my mother's, at her worship, had been a dove's. My hands clenched over

18

the oar grip, and the sweat that dripped from my forehead was not in the weather, for there was coolness on the water, and the still light shone.

Then at last the old man we called the Bear ceased to talk and waited. I said, "It has come to me, old man. The knowledge that I would rather die in the attempt than live as I have for a year gone on living. Breath without freedom is dead in the lungs. It stinks in the throat. Up to now"—it was hard saying, but I had to inform him; though possibly, it comes to me now, he knew—"up to now I have owned a shield." He nodded. I said, "It served as my armor against madness; it guarded me from the helpless thoughts of those who dare to hope. But——" I was breathing more slowly, and the racing tide of my blood had calmed. He nodded again. I went on, "But that itself is, I see, a sort of madness. I do not know how others in the past have felt concerning slavery. I do not see now—though in the past I thought I had seen—how any man born could be a good slave. A good slave!" I laughed—only a little. And he was laughing as well. "Well, well, then," I said. "You have my apology for being born a fool."

He said, "Wait. Wait, now. I will tell Diarno, on the bench ahead of me." And he nodded once more, slowly, as if we had all the time in the world; as if the sand in the hourglasses, the water in the water clocks, were not falling and floating. I felt the same. I felt that the same light would come in through those ports forever; that until we willed it, the dawn with its cries and alarms, its crowing of the pet fighting cocks the officers kept in cages for their amusement, would never come. So I sat back, watching my hands on my oar grip; they were lightly clenching now, and for the first time since I had come to this place—save in broken dreams—I was at peace.

And yet it was not a safe plan. No soldier alive whose existence depended on it would have thought it foolproof. We had no maps scrolled out, no definite campaign deploying this man here, that one there. We had a battered multitude upon whom we might, if the gods smiled, depend; Jason in his magic ship had safer protection! And as for our men, they were all in chains. Yet I must tell this too: the structure of the ship, its heaviness and substance around me, did not seem to be there. It was as if the known world were weightless and also as if I could, a little, see through it into something beyond. I lifted my head and mumbled what I could recall of the prayers my mother had always made to her important gods. As I did so I was astonished to see the circles of iron still clamping my wrists. They seemed to have no place there; to be figments of my thought, unimportant and not encumbering me. Ahead, the old Bear had succeeded in wakening Diarno; I could hear them in low converse. I could make out their bare outlines in that light.

The wonder of that light! Sometimes it comes back to me at untoward moments; when I am only walking down my village street, an old man now, and with my mind on something else—there it is, quick and flashing like the look you catch, slanting, in the eye of a child; but sustained and lasting long. I do not think it is a simple light to find. And yet it comes most simply and when it is not expected. It has appeared to me often and clearly since.

I sat in it then and waited; and presently, in the timeless slowness of all around me, the Bear leaned back once more and murmured. "Now." Only the word; it was enough. For I stood, crouching as high as I could in my chains, and gave a great roar fit to bring down all the Roman false gods in a black-winged fury. At the selfsame moment the Bear stood and roared at the top of his lungs; and smaller Diarno, beyond him, was upon his feet, clutching as we did at the chains, shaking them and calling.

I tell you it was a sound. All around us the half-sleeping men stirred and jangled their chains, cursed and reviled us—for such a noise brings out the most grim, whimsical side of overseers and officers and captain. Then, when I saw the overseer's lamp, this time come bobbing in haste down the stair, I stopped the noise and sat once more. He had seen me, no doubt of it; I was the last of us three to slump back in my chains. Around us all tumult ceased also, as the overseer, lamp flashing high, pounded down the aisle way. Through near-shut eyes I could see him as he raised the whip in his right hand—they are strong, these Roman half-servants, and they have their own sense of rough justice. Yet his voice seemed to me thin and unworldly.

The whip fell upon my shoulders. It fell, and fell, and fell again. Through the lashing, through his voice, angry and full of its self-importance, I watched the light which did not alter. And surely the gods are wondrous when they arrive, for I only pitied him. To be sure I pitied him even a shade more when the Bear, rising in front of me, reached and managed to drag the overseer within a tremendous grip of forearms. But that had been in the plan, to anger this overseer—in a year you know a man well, at least on the outer side, and can gauge what he will or will not do—and it was falling out as it should have. I must tell, too, that I was not surprised. This overseer was the same who, a month before, had tortured the man on the bench in front of Diarno until he drove that one to madness; there is rough justice in all of life, it seems. And fortunately the Bear had clutched him in the proper position for breaking a neck, so that there was no outcry. The lamp had been knocked down; it burned for a little and then went out with a splutter and some mild smoking. After that we worked in the shadows, while the light through the sweep ports stayed as it had before. All along the banks of crouching men it went its way, touching an eye here, a curve of knotted shoulder there. A great gentle light; remembering my mother's gods, I wished the soul of the overseer well on its journey through the dark underworld. When we were done with him in the shadows and had his short-sword, little Diarno said in the voice of an agitated reed, "Hit with the blade, strike off your chains!"

But the Bear's voice was strong and reaching as the duumvir's drums above deck. "We will not blunt the blade on our chains, Diarno." The Bear was standing as high as he could in his chains; he held the sword, it glittered in the calm light. He spoke to the banks of rowers; all were awake now, turning and watching, waiting. "I have the overseer's sword!" he called. "If we stand together—all of us pulling to the limit of our strength—we can break these benches. We outnumber overseers and soldiers. I will walk up

22

the stairs in the lead, using the sword, so that if there is more blood-letting, mine will be the blood first spilled. And now, come!" Suddenly his voice rang and was greater than the duumvir's drums. "Stand, pull for life and freedom as did those slaves under the decks at Actium!"

Of course it had been done before. Slaves in the galleys had pulled up their benches in the past. Yet for so long had it been a blind and empty dream to these men that, as the Bear's words ceased ringing, there was at first only an echoing growl and mutter among them—but I was standing, straining on the chains; Diarno was standing. Then I could see a scrawny-necked, knob-shouldered wreck of a man in front of Diarno, also standing; and the murmur was growing to a shout, and more were upon their feet. In the wood of the benches to which the chains were attached came a slight shudder. Now the strain on the circles of iron around my wrists was intolerable, as though it would cut my hands off. I knew every man was feeling it, and there was no time for cheering or shouting; only for the vast, concerted effort.

And then with a rending crash a bench came up, splintering and cracking as it came; and another; and just when I had felt that my bench was of iron rooted to stand forever, the heavy but rotted and sea-water-spoiled timber yielded, groaned, and my hands flew high, the chains jangling together as the bench wood flew to strike my back with jagged edges. I noted no pain; only that the light was as steady, as full and serene as it had been. I marveled a little that these benches, built to withstand just such an insurrection, had finally broken; yet to tell the truth, I marveled more at the serenity of the light. For in those moments—as, all around me, more benches cracked, split, as more men stood to their full height—I felt that any man alive can do anything he truly wishes to do. Often I still feel that. It is a feeling beyond jubilation. It has to do with calm, with strength, with a silent light.

We were a strange, bedraggled army—dragging stumps of benches from our arms, wedges of wood that swung heavily, we stood high and free—walking into the aisle, clambering down from the ports, leaving those accursed oars. We were a strange awkward army; but there was strength in us as fierce as any army at Thermopylae. And as more and more of us stepped into the aisle, and as there was noise above decks—a cry, a shout, the running of feet, the signals that the officers had heard us and would meet us above the hatchway—Diarno and I took our places just behind the Bear at the head of this slow-footed, freedom-breathing army. The sword glittered in the Bear's right hand. The chains that swung from his wrist did not impede the clean strength of that hand. Chains, too, could be weapons; it came to me that all of us were well-armed. Just behind me a dark little man with one eye said, peering forward and up to the hatchway stairs, "I am not crying from fear, friend. It's not fear! But I had never thought to be standing upright again. I had never thought it!"

We were moving forward now, the Bear, then Diarno and I, then the rest at our backs. As we reached the hatchway steps, carrying our chains, the duumvir's drums sounded out above us. The tip of

24

the sword in the Bear's right hand reached into the light pouring down those steps. It was like an answer to the drums. I knew, watching it, that soon the drums would be silenced; yet, though I had always, as I've said, hated the duumvir and the idea of time-keeping drums most of all, yet now there was no hate in me. It was past hate. It was very quiet. It was justice and need. Watching the Bear, too, as we climbed on—there they were, ringing the hatchway, a dozen or twenty soldiers, their swords ready, their armor on, their faces set in that cascade of brilliant light—watching the Bear as I also watched these soldiers, I had the thought that he would have made a great gladiator. But then he was a farmer and not a believer in that sort of fighting. He was a man and no skilled beast. That was part of the reason why they could not stop us. They had precision and the art of arms on their side. We had nothing but ourselves and one sword and the chains and the bench ends—and our terrible need.

The first soldiers leaped; the Bear swung his sword; I was attacked from the left, and was flailing with my chains, with all my released strength. From the hatchway poured the rest of our men, streaming up and up, pouring out to cover the deck—even then, in the maelstrom of blows and blood and shouts and the swarming blindness of battle, I noted how the vast light shone. It was not a soft light. It was gentle, but very strong. It seemed to me then that it stood beyond battle, beyond the raging shadows on the deck boards, as though it contained and cupped the final truth of battle and all man's striving. We fought on.

They fought well, I suppose, those soldiers. Their captain—he was astoundingly young—was very valiant. He would gladly have died rather than bear the ignominy of enduring an escape of the galley slaves from a ship under his command. Yet they had fought one battle that day and had been in a storm afterward. I have thought much, since then; I know how they felt; I can, perhaps, sympathize. We were too many for them; at the first there was bloodshed, and some of our men went down, and some of theirs. But even then, at the first, you could tell how it would end. Yet there was a mystery past all this; I think somehow that they felt it too. I think it slowed their sword arms and gave pause to their trained rushes and bitter sallies.

Later—oh, it seemed much later, though it appeared to me that the light in the sky would stand forever, and that whatever dawn came after it would be like no other dawn yet seen—we had conquered them. We had bound them hand and foot; had laid the bodies of the dead apart for decent burial. And, though you would think the utmost vengeance would live among our men and that, even with the Bear commanding us, we would not leave a soldier or an overseer alive—this was not so. It, too, was part of the mystery. I have no easy words for it. Yet it was there, moving among us, bound into the light which seemed part of our bones and bellies. I am an old man now, yet even today I have not answered the questions that came to me then as, after the battle, after the silencing of the duumvir's drums, I walked with the Bear on deck. We stood in the stern, near that high-curved sweep of wood. Its shadow was a swan's throat on the hushed water. And again I smelled the land—it smelled of olive trees and beautiful darkness; it was not far off past this deck.

After we had rested a little and before the morning came, we would finish striking off all of our chains and would row for shore. That had been decided. But now the questions leaped on my tongue.

"You were right," I said. "I have never smelled land like this one. Where are we, then, old Bear?"

He was leaning on the bulwark, watching the light on the water. He said, "I have smelled this land before in other seasons. I could not forget it, Voldi. I came here with my father when I was very young. There"—he gestured—"is the edge of Egypt; and this, before us, is Palestine. And we are near Jaffa, off the Palestine coast." He plucked at his chin and stared into the sky. You could see where most of the light came from. It came from a single star. I remember its light. Where are there words to say it all? It was a young rose, and the fire in the blood of youth, and the new air of morning, and the end of countless years. "There was a town, Bethlehem, they called it the House of God. They waited for a sign in the sky—I remember well. The sign would tell them of the birth of a king." He stopped; then went on. "Voldi, that star is the sign; I think it hangs near the town, near that Bethlehem."

I did not answer. I could tell that he could answer no more of my questions, so I asked no more then. We only went on looking at the star. Sometimes I think I still see it—that it has never gone out.

29

Paul Darcy Boles
with joy,
Atlanta/1980